ENDORS

"John Bell's book, 'Life, Life and More Life,' is a breath of fresh air which will empower each reader to embrace the fullness of Christ's provision for abundance. Your heart will be challenged and your eyes opened to the enemy's tactics so you can overcome and receive all the blessings heaven intended. Thank you John for this powerful devotional that will bring freedom and hope to many."

Jane Hamon, Vision Church @ Christian International, Author of: Dreams and Visions, The Deborah Company, The Cyrus Decree, Discernment

"This is a brilliant book! Like John Bell, this book is full of Life. Everywhere he goes, Life breaks out around him. You are holding in your hand a powerful tool that will lead you on a journey to life in all its fullness."

Joshua Fowler, Author of Daily Decrees, Awake the World

"John Bell's book will motivate, encourage and propel you into abundant life in Christ. It's filled with truth that will help you overcome anything holding you back. As I read it, I was personally touched and deeply inspired. God helped John overcome terminal cancer and the same God is going to empower you. John will lead you in daily prayer and declarations with God's life transforming word. I know this book will deeply impact many areas of your life."

Matt Sorger, Prophetic Minister, Author and TV Host

"In current Christian culture, we generally equate the word "Life" with the ending of abortion. But life is something that should be declared and heralded throughout the earth from the cradle to the grave. My friend John Bell, having been faced himself with the reality of life being taken from him, is a life herald. I've met many people in my Christian walk, but I've met very few that live the constant message of life and hope like John does. I pray that as you read, you become infused with a deep desire to declare life everywhere you go."

Anthony Medina, Founder, Hope Fires International

"From the moment we met in Chicago years ago, John has overflowed with joy and life! I am certain His book, 'Life, Life and More Life' will challenge you to live life to the fullest, regardless of the situations and circumstances you face. Choose life today."

Joan Hunter, Author and Healing Evangelist, TV Host of Miracles Happen

"I have known John for years and one thing is certain, John is an incredible encourager. He inspires faith and confidence in the God who redeemed his life from the jaws of cancer. John walks in the favor and blessing of God because he listens and follows all that God tells him to do. 'Life, life and more life,' is an amazing book filled with prophetic insight, practical teaching and opportunities for application that will change your life."

Sue Sinclair, Prophet, CWM Ministries

"Hold onto your hats, John is coming! John always lives his life full on, full power, abandoned to love. We first met John when he was fighting cancer. What a journey that was. John has brought so much of Father's sunshine into our lives. We love the life in him, we love his integrity, we love his enormous heart of compassion, we love his mad sense of adventure, we love the energy, we love the incisive prophetic nature of his seeing heart, we love his longing for unity. And you will love this book."

Nick and Linda Holt, England

LIFE, LIFE
and
More *Life*

The Power of Declaring Life
in the Most Challenging
of Circumstances

JOHN BELL

Life, Life and More Life
The Power of Declaring Life in the Most Challenging of Circumstances
John Bell

Published by:

Mary Ethel

Mary Ethel Eckard
Frisco, Texas

To contact the author:
johnbellHCL@outlook.com
www.hclministries.com

ISBN (Print): 978-1-7338233-4-0

DEDICATION

This book is dedicated to all who have walked out life with Susie and me. It is dedicated to our teams in Colombia, our spiritual children, the people we serve, and those who support us so generously to help us do all we do in the name of Jesus. I have received life and encouragement from you all in so many ways. This book is for each of you. May you receive life as others are encouraged by the contents of this book.

Special Thanks

To those who have walked before me; the amazing mentors in my life who have challenged me to grow and stand firm in my identity and authority as an ambassador of Christ.

To my beautiful wife Susie who has stood by me every step of the way and accepted the prophetic in me and all the challenges that can bring.

To Lynn and Les for persevering with me in the early days, seeing potential in me, and leading me to Christ.

To ministry leaders in the United States who have encouraged me to release my voice and be a blessing to the wider church - not only in the United States of America, but also in the nations.

CONTENTS

PART THREE: ABUNDANT LIFE

INTRODUCTION

They say that life is a journey and that the journey is far more important than the final destination. My question is, what if it feels like there is no life in the journey? What if you simply want to arrive at the destination and skip over the journey because it is too traumatic, disappointing, and painful? Perhaps hearing part of my story will encourage you to step into life's journey with renewed vigor.

At the age of 28, I was driving home from work when my stomach perforated, and I began losing units and units of blood. My life flashed before me. Within a matter of hours, I was diagnosed with terminal cancer and given a life expectancy of 90 days. No 28-year-old should have to face the possibility of their own death, and no 28-year-old should have to think about and plan for their own funeral.

Though I had given my heart to Christ in the final year of my university studies, life was empty. There was a dark hole and a void I tried unsuccessfully to fill with almost everything. In the world's eyes, I was a success. I worked as an IT professional in the industry, I had a nice car and a great place to live. I was always well-loved and liked, but in reality, my life was a mess. I was empty and somewhat lonely, looking for life and love in all the wrong places.

In the midst of the battle with cancer, the Lord gave me a second chance, healed me from a terminal illness, and gave me a mandate from

Psalm 118:17. "I will not die but live and declare the good works the Lord has done." This supernatural impartation of life was not expected nor planned. It came out of the blue and radically changed me. I began to live on fire for Him.

The Lord used cancer, a terminal diagnosis, and a near death experience to turn my life around. He used it to give me passion, and to show me the journey ahead, which was, in reality, no longer living for self but surrendering my life to Him. It involved dying to myself, both physically and spiritually, letting go of everything.

It's ironic that when we surrender our lives to Him, when we no longer live selfishly to fill our own needs, He gives our life back to us more completely and abundantly... with nothing missing, nothing lacking, and nothing broken. Giving myself to Jesus is where I found my true self. Life has never been the same since that miraculous healing, recovery, and turnaround.

Even this book is written in answer to the mandate given to me by the Lord. I'm alive. I lived and did not die, now I have a job to do. I'm here to declare the good works the Lord has done! My prayer and hope for you is that you will find life. Maybe you are looking for life in the wrong places. Maybe it is time to give your life to Jesus, to surrender all areas to Him. I promise that when you give over your life to Him, when you die to self, you *will* find life in the process.

This devotional is an adventure in God's Word. As you journey toward abundant life over the next 30 days, I pray you will discover life in all its fullness. I decree and declare life, life, and more life over you right now, in the mighty name of Jesus. Amen.

PART ONE

REALITY OF LIFE

"For you created my inmost being; you knit me together in my mother's womb. I praise you because I am fearfully and wonderfully made."
Psalm 139:13

DAY 1

. . . .

Accepting Reality

Jesus said, "The thief comes only to steal and kill and destroy;
I have come that they may have life and have it to the full."
John 10:10

The words above show us clearly that Jesus came to give us life, and life in abundance. A life with nothing missing, nothing lacking, and nothing broken. A life that is full of perfect peace. My guess is that just by picking up this devotional guide, you have a sense that there's more life for you, and you are not living your life to its full capacity.

One of the ways we have access to this abundant life is by accepting the reality of where we are right now, by accepting the reality of what we are facing, the situations, and circumstances we find ourselves in, and by accepting the way in which we approach these things. Most people will tell you that accepting the reality is the first step of the process of learning how to live an abundant life.

So that's my encouragement to you today. Begin to take stock, to do an inventory, and ask yourself the deeper question, "Where do I find myself right now? Am I living the abundant life? Where are things in my life that are not where I want them to be?"

In Psalm 37:4, the Lord clearly says that He gives us the desires of our heart. Maybe it's time for you to begin learning to express the desires of your heart to Him in prayer. Maybe it's time to begin talking with Him again and sharing with Him those deeper desires.

The Lord wants you to live an abundant life. He wants you to be able to reach your full potential. The way we do that is by choosing to accept our reality. Choose to accept your reality today. Choose to be real with yourself and honest with Him in conversation about where you are, how you feel, and the situations and circumstances that are not quite meeting the mark in your life.

By the end of this devotional series, you will be encouraged with many topics, ideas, and tools in order to find yourself living the full life that the Lord has intended for you.

PRAYER

Father,

Your Word says that we will know the truth and the truth will set us free. Today I surrender before You, asking You to lead and guide me into the full truth. Help me identify and accept the reality I am living in and give me access to abundant life. I believe You are the God of life, of nothing missing, nothing lacking, and nothing broken. As I begin this journey into life in all its fullness, I start by declaring my desire to receive abundant life. In the mighty name of Jesus. Amen.

The Quest of Abundant Life
· · · · · · · · · · · · ·
ACCEPTING REALITY

Are you living the abundant life?

What are the areas of your life that seem to be less than God's best for you?

Read Psalm 37:4. What are the desires of your heart?

Are your desires in alignment with God's plans and purposes for your life?

Read Jeremiah 29:11-13. Pen a prayer expressing your hearts desires to God. Invite Him to realign the desires of your heart to His desires for you.

DAY 2

. . . .

Curse of Comparison

"I praise you because I am fearfully and wonderfully made.
Your works are wonderful, I know that full well."
Psalm 139:14

The root of comparison starts when we see the things we need or want and do not have. It's easy to make comparison to those who appear to be more successful, better looking, or even a better person. Yet, it's impossible to be content in who we are and how we were created if we are constantly comparing ourselves to others.

Psalm 139:14 challenges us to believe we are fearfully and wonderfully made by our Creator, Father God. We are reminded that He loves us, and He is pleased with and delighted in us. This verse is a helpful declaration to make when we are worried about who we are and insecure in our identity. It's time to stop selling ourselves short. It's time to stop upsetting the Father by believing we can be better by looking or behaving like someone else.

The curse of comparison is like a cancer. It eats you from the inside out. A heart of gratitude is the greatest weapon to stop or kill the curse of comparison. We give thanks to God for those things we do have, and we bless those people who appear to have more than we do.

Today is the day to take a deep breath and rest in the assurance that we are great just the way we are. The Father has beautiful plans for us, amazing dreams and ideas for our lives. If we simply relax in the confidence that we are created the way we are and realize that we are good enough, then the curse of comparison will no longer affect us.

PRAYER

Lord,

We thank You for creating us fearfully and wonderfully. We acknowledge that Your works are wonderful, and we know that full well. Today we confess to You that we have compared ourselves and felt inadequate. We ask You today, Holy Spirit, to pour out Your love and remind us that we are wonderfully and fearfully made. We are made in Your image. Amen.

The Quest of Abundant Life
. . . .
CURSE OF COMPARISON

Rewind your thoughts over the past 48 hours. In that time period, recall how many times you compared yourself, your life, and your situation in life to others. Recall the situation and circumstances that took you down the road of comparison.

Seek God's forgiveness in these thoughts and comparisons.

Rehearse the blessings God has bestowed to you over the same 48-hour time period. Pen a prayer of thanksgiving to Him, focusing on the "haves" rather than the "have-nots."

Read Proverbs 14:30. How does comparison and envy impact the quality of life?

Scripture teaches that we are to "give thanks in all circumstances." Thanksgiving breeds contentment and abolishes the curse of comparison. A heart of peace is the fruit of contentment. Revisit Proverbs 14:30. What impact does a heart of peace have on the quality of life?

DAY 3

· ·

Depth of Disappointment

"When the righteous cry for help, the Lord hears
and delivers them out of all their troubles.
The Lord is near to the brokenhearted and saves the crushed in spirit."
Psalm 34:17-18

Disappointment is defined as unmet expectations. It would be unrealistic to claim that we can live a life free of disappointment. When our unrealistic expectations of ourselves or others are not met, we often find ourselves disappointed, leading to a broken heart and a crushed spirit, which, in turn, paralyzes us from moving forward.

It's important to accept the reality that we may have disappointment in certain areas of our life and to identify those areas so we can move forward.

In the scripture above, the Lord is clear about how we are to deal with disappointments. We are to bring them to Him and cry out for help, knowing He will hear and deliver us from all our troubles. The Lord Jesus does not want us living in disappointment. He wants to inject us with hope so we can stand up and move forward. Perhaps He wants us to take risks in the very same areas in which we have been disappointed in the past.

It's time to try again, to give it another go, to shake off the disappointments from the past and move with excitement and encouragement into the things of the future. Do not remain in disappointment but take unmet expectations to the cross and leave them at the altar. Allow the Lord to inject hope, which is the opposite of disappointment.

Today I speak hope over you; hope that helps you meet expectations and hope that delivers you from all disappointment.

PRAYER

Lord,

Today I acknowledge I have been disappointed in certain areas of my life. I acknowledge that disappointment has resulted in me becoming stagnant and paralyzed, not wanting to move out of disappointment and move forward. Lord Jesus, thank You for empowering me to move on, to stand up, and to give it another go. Thank You that when I cry out for help, You hear me and deliver me from my troubles. Thank You for being close to the brokenhearted and the crushed in spirit. Thank You for saving me from my disappointments. In the mighty name of Jesus. Amen.

The Quest of Abundant Life
· · · · · · · · · · · ·
DEPTH OF DISAPPOINTMENT

Has the weight of disappointment rendered you motionless or stuck? What are these disappointments? Write them below.

Read Psalm 66:8-12. The writer of this Psalm spoke from a place of disappointment and defeat. How did he turn his perspective from loss and disappointment to seeing life through God's eyes?

Psalm 66:12 tells us that after all the disappointment and trials, the Lord "brought him to a place of abundance." How can God use disappointment in your life to grow and mature you?

With hindsight vision, things are seen more clearly. If you are in a season of disappointment, ask God to give you His perspective in your situation so you can see what He is doing behind the scenes of your life. Lean into Him for wisdom and understanding.

For a word of encouragement and to battle discouragement, read Psalm 20. As you read, pray this scripture over yourself and others who need a prayer of hope and victory in the quest to abundant life.

DAY 4

· ·

Fearing Failure

"For the spirit God gave us does not make us timid
but gives us power, love, and self-discipline."
2 Timothy 1:7

It's ironic that the fear of failure can stop us from trying to succeed. The words above remind us that we have not been given a spirit of fear, but we have been given the spirit of God, which gives us a sound mind, power, love, and self-discipline. It's important to note that there is no place for fear to reside within us because we have been created as more than a conqueror in Christ Jesus.

Are you dealing with fear? Are you failing to achieve the things you desire simply because you have felt they would not go right? Fear stops us from moving forward; fear stops us from being the person God created us to be. Fear is the very thing that derails us from the plans and purposes the Lord has ordained for us from the beginning of time. Fear can also create physical symptoms in the body. Most illnesses have a root based in fear.

The Lord desires to heal and release us from the spirit of fear. His perfect love casts out all fear, so when His perfect love floods into our heart, mind and life, there simply will be no place for fear to reside. He desires to set us free and to lavish His love upon us.

Be encouraged today as the Spirit of the Lord injects hope into you, encouraging you and increasing your level of faith that the things He has placed before you, you are able to do. Not only will you do them, but you will succeed and even over deliver. He is the One who has called you to do these very things. You are more successful, loved, welcomed, and worthy than you realize. You have a greater ability to achieve your plans than you believe. Open your eyes and heart to receive the powerful and unconditional love of Jesus.

PRAYER

Father God,

When I dwell in Your perfect love, there is no place for fear. So, I say today, "Spirit of fear, you are no longer welcome to control, limit, or stop me from doing the things the Lord has called me to. You no longer have permission to operate in my life." Lord, thank You that I am empowered to move forward and no longer allow the Spirit of fear to paralyze me as in the past. I am a new creation and I have been given a sound mind. In the name of Jesus. Amen.

The Quest of Abundant Life
. . . .
FEARING FAILURE

Has your life been hindered by fear? What are your greatest fears? List those below.

Confess these fears to the Lord. Simply ask Him to remove the spirit of fear from your heart and to replace it with His spirit of power, love, and self-discipline.

John mentioned that we are "more than conquerors in Christ Jesus." To see how this helps overcome the battle against fear, read Romans 8:31-39.

What two truths stand out to you that help you understand that faith in God is greater than the fear of life?

Today is a great day to step on the head of fear and take a step toward your future. What is one thing you can do today to overcome fear?

DAY 5

. . . .

Walk of Worry

"Do not be anxious about anything, but in every situation by prayer
and petition with thanksgiving present your request to God."
Philippians 4:6

Some translations say, "Do not worry about anything." Fear and worry often go hand in hand. Worry is not as obvious and in your face as the spirit of fear, but it is equally as toxic and dangerous. It starts small, it's subtle, and it comes as a thief in the night. It is important to acknowledge worry the moment it starts so we can pull it out at the root. We need to make sure we do not allow our hearts to become worried.

But how? The scripture above says that instead of worrying about anything, we are to turn our worries into prayers and petitions. We can choose to see the things that worry us from a different angle and perspective. We can choose to see challenges rather than difficulties; we can choose to see opportunities rather than problems.

When we tackle the issue of living free from fear, we also find that we begin to live free from worry. Look at your situations and circumstances today. Be real. Acknowledge that worry has crept in and deal with that worry by praying this prayer:

PRAYER

Father God,

Thank You that You are a God who gives instructions, telling us to pray and bring our petitions before You rather than worry. Right now, in the name of Jesus, I pause and ask You to reveal to me, by the power of your Holy Spirit, any area of my life in which I am worried and maybe didn't realize until now. I give You these concerns and worries and ask You to make a way where there seems to be no way. You are the God of miraculous outcomes, who has a perfect plan for my life. Therefore, today I declare my trust in You, and there is no longer any place for me to worry. In the name of Jesus. Amen.

The Quest of Abundant Life
. . . .
WALK OF WORRY

Proverbs 12:25 tells us that an anxious heart, or a heart of worry, weighs a man down. Where in your life have you fallen captive to worry and feel weighted down?

List your top five worries and concerns. Next, beside each item listed, write a sentence prayer for each one, inviting the Holy Spirit to work all things out for His glory. When the worries and concerns try to return, release them again through prayer, giving them to the Lord.

The opposite of worry is peace. Worry happens when we allow our thoughts to get out of control and then those thoughts control us. Read Romans 8:6. What is the by-product of a mind that is controlled by the Spirit of God?

Romans 12:2 reminds us of the importance of renewing and retraining our minds. Learning to control the thoughts requires intentionality. Read Philippians 4:8 and list the things we are told to think about that will help us escape worry.

Faith and trust in God are other remedies for worry. In Matthew 6:25-34, Jesus reminds us that we are His creation, and it is His responsibility to look after our needs. How does this truth help reframe your thought processes?

DAY 6

. . . .

Identity Investigation

"And I will be a Father to you, and you shall be sons
and daughters to me, says the Lord Almighty."
2 Corinthians 6:18

The question of sonship is a big topic in the body of Christ. As we begin to investigate our identity of who we are, how we were created, and who we belong to, the topic of father-ship always comes up.

Maybe you know who you are and are secure in your relationship as a son or daughter of the Father and the Most High King. But perhaps this is an area you have questioned, and it has caused you to be held back and not fulfill your God-given potential.

To be a son or daughter of God means to have the ability or position to receive the full unconditional love of the Father. This Father is not like an earthly father. He is not angry, distant, or expecting anything in return. He does not withhold his love, affection, or provision because of your bad behavior. His love is pure. 1 Corinthians 13 tell us that His love for us is patient and kind, and it always protects, trusts, hopes, and perseveres so that we are continually drawn to Him. His love never fails us. His love casts all fear out of us.

When we discover who we are, how we were created, and who we were created by, we are released into the abundant life, which is life in its fullness. We can rest in the knowledge and security that we are deeply loved. As we learn to operate as a son or daughter, not as a slave, we fully begin to come into our God-given identity.

PRAYER

Father,

Thank You that You call us sons and daughters. We come before You today from that place and position. Today I accept Your unconditional love and come into a full and complete knowledge of who You are as Father, Daddy, God. Thank You that Your love for me is unconditional, never ending, and never changing. It's the same yesterday, today and tomorrow. When everything around me feels like sinking sand, I can stand on You, my solid rock, knowing who I am and who I belong to. Amen.

The Quest of Abundant Life
·············
IDENTITY INVESTIGATION

One of the quests for abundant life is understanding our true identity. Not who others say we are, not who we think we are, but who God says we are and who He created us to be. Are you a child of God? Eternal life with God begins when you confess your sins to Him, seek His forgiveness, and receive His gift of salvation. (Romans 6:26, Romans 10:9). Have you sought and received this gift? If yes, pen a prayer of thanksgiving! If no, pause and pray, seeking God's forgiveness and His gift of salvation. Then write today's day below as a remembrance of the day you received eternal life with God and became His son or daughter.

Our quest for identity is found in the search of scripture. Read Ephesians 3:16-19 and 1 John 3:1. As you read, journal the words or phrases that help you understand more fully your identity that comes from being a child of God. Why do you think these words or phrases minister to you so deeply?

Find Psalm 139 in your Bible. Begin at verse 1 and read until a word or phrase resonates with your heart. Stop reading and write this word or phrase in your journal. Meditate on it. Understand that the Holy Spirit highlighted those words or phrases to you and He wants to use these to minister to you as truth toward your identity in Him.

God created you with a specific purpose and plan. Read Jeremiah 1:5. He designed you with skills, talents, and interests that set your lifepath in motion toward your destiny. List below your skills, talents and interests.

If you are willing, submit these natural strengths, skills, and abilities to the Father. Ask Him to empower those strengths with His supernatural power and giftings and to pair them with the spiritual gifts He has for you, as His child. Receive His anointing and authority to step into your true identity and destiny, His child who is called to change the world by bringing glory to Him.

DAY 7

. . . .

Death and Disease

"Have I not commanded you? Be strong and courageous.
Do not be afraid; do not be discouraged, for the Lord
your God will be with you wherever you go."
Joshua 1:9

This verse literally means that, wherever you go, whatever your situation or circumstance, in the middle of death and disease, God is with you. It's a promise from scripture we need to be reminded of especially when we face difficulties.

Death and disease are topics I can speak into with all authority and clarity. I'm reminded of a time in life when I received a terminal diagnosis of cancer accompanied with a life expectancy of 90 days. This verse became alive to me as I was reminded not to be afraid or discouraged but to walk in strength and courage. This may sound harder than it seems but meditating on scripture and God's promises empowered faith within me to rise above the fear and discouragement.

You may not be facing a terminal diagnosis, but there may be a spiritual disease around you. Perhaps you've lost a loved one, or you've become aware of the death of a dream. Perhaps it's the reality of something you wanted to see come to fruition, but that did not take place. Perhaps you are living in a place of discouragement right now.

Today I speak life into those dead circumstances and situations. I speak life into your heart, your mind, and your emotions. I speak life over every single area where fear and discouragement try to render you dead, in the mighty name of Jesus.

Do not be afraid or discouraged, for the Lord your God will be with you wherever you go. It's time to fix your eyes upon Him again, to receive abundant life from Him, to stand on His Word and meditate on the power of scripture. It's time to receive the abundant life the Lord has for you today.

PRAYER

Lord Jesus,

I thank You that Your Word encourages me to be strong and courageous. I confess to You that in my own strength, I feel weak and afraid. I choose to stand upon Your Word which is true and does not return void. Today I receive Your strength and courage. I receive from You a spirit of confidence and not a spirit of fear. Thank You that You are with me wherever I go, whether it be good, challenging, or bad, You are with me. In in the mighty name of Jesus. Amen.

The Quest of Abundant Life
· · · · · · · · · · · ·
DEATH AND DISEASE

James 3:1-12 speaks of the power of our words and how they direct our path. Our words have the power to create or destroy life. If you were to measure your words, would you say they are used more for creation or destruction? What can you do to get your words back on the track of creating life?

One of my favorite verses is Romans 4:17, which says God gives life to the dead and calls things that are not as though they were. In other words, God speaks life into dead places and brings resurrection and restoration. What dead places do you need to resurrect with the power of positive words and truth?

Find and write the verse from Proverbs 16:24 in your journal. What is one advantage of using positive words when speaking of death and disease?

We learn in Isaiah 55:10 that God's Word, spoken from our lips, will not return void but will accomplish the purpose for which God sends it. Declare into the atmosphere, using your aloud voice, that the dry bones of your situation and circumstances are receiving new life. Journal your prayer below and add today's date so you can track God's work in bringing life.

Part of living an abundant life is understanding the power of words, not only in your own life, but in the lives of others. Look for opportunities today to be an encouragement to someone, to pray for someone, to use your words to speak life. Allow your words to clear the path for someone else to see the love of Christ shine through you.

DAY 8

. . . .

Thoughts and Feelings

"Then you will know the truth and the truth will set you free."
John 8:32

When we find ourselves a few degrees off balance because of the storms, circumstances, and situations of life, we often find that our thoughts and feelings begin to drive and lead us. They become the things that speak to us the loudest, and often end up being the very things that lead us to make bad decisions. We must remember that thoughts and feelings are not always the truth.

As we continue this journey for the quest of abundant life, and in our pursuit of freedom, we need to remember that the Word of God sets us back to true north. His truth sets us back in the reality of life, faith, and perspective.

Have you made decisions based on thoughts or feelings that have not led to positive consequences? Sometimes even our identity is made up of the thoughts and feelings we have about ourselves or about what others have spoken over us. We must remember, and never forget, that Satan lies to us about who we are and whose we are. He plants thoughts in our minds in an attempt to stir our emotions and cause us to say and do things that are outside of our true character and identity.

It is time to remember the truth of what the Lord says in scripture about standing for truth and recognizing the lies of Satan. He warns us in scripture that Satan prowls around like a roaring lion, looking for someone to devour. Remembering this helps us discern the difference between reacting because of our thoughts and feelings and discerning when the enemy is stirring us to get us off track. The Word of God warns us of enemy tactics. The Word of God leads us to abundant life.

My heart for you today is to find the truth that counter the lies. The truth will set you free and then you will have access to life, life and more life.

PRAYER

Father,

I surrender my thoughts and feelings to You today. Thank You that when I search for the truth, I will find it, and it will set me free. I acknowledge that I am honest and truthful in saying that in my past, thoughts and feelings have often led, directed, and guided me into places I did not wish to go. Today I make a commitment to allow Your truth to lead and guide me, therefore putting me on a path to fruition, a path that leads me in the direction of the purpose and plan You have for my life. In the mighty name of Jesus. Amen.

The Quest of Abundant Life
. . . .
THOUGHTS AND FEELINGS

Ezekiel 28:11-19 gives the account of how Satan went from being an angel in the service of God to an enemy of God. It's an interesting read. Before the creation of the earth, Satan set out to war against God. When God created mankind in Genesis 1, Satan was on the earth; he set in place an ambush to destroy man, who is created in God's image. To read more about Satan's fall, turn to Isaiah 14:12-15. Commit today to walk with God and not fall prey to Satan's scheme to render you lifeless, useless, and voiceless.

Jesus warns us against the schemes of Satan in John 8:42-47. Journal the different ways mentioned within these verses of how Satan tries to trip up God's children.

The lies of Satan, whether spoken by others or planted in our minds, can deter us from walking in obedience to the ways of God. But as children of God, we have been given the Spirit of Truth, the Holy Spirit who resides within us. (John 16:13). To dispel the lies of Satan and to overcome his attempt to stir negative emotions, we commit our way to understanding God's truth. What are the main areas in life where you are tripped up or triggered?

Ask the Holy Spirit to direct you to scripture that will help you overcome the habit or tendency of reacting to these triggers or situations. Wisdom and truth from scripture equip you to respond rather than to react. Choose to walk in truth and wisdom. Search scripture for both.

Bookmark this page. As you walk through the rest of this devotional, come back to this page and write down additional areas where you have been tripped up or triggered. Keep a log of the areas of life where the lies of the enemy try to ambush you and get you off course. Each time you add something to this list, pray over everything on this page! Set a wall of protection around your heart, soul, and spirit so the lies of the enemy are deflected and bounce back on him.

. . . .

Requiring Resources

"And my God will meet all your needs according to
the riches of His glory in Christ Jesus."
Philippians 4:19

This is an area I know all too well. Being a missionary required me to step away from a regularly paying job and trust that the Lord would provide for all our needs.

Maybe you are requiring resources right now and the lack of resources has led to you to feeling that you do not have access to the abundant life.

The challenge today is to trust the promise, "God will meet all of your needs according to the riches of His glory." The question is, what are your needs?

The Bible says that the Lord takes care of the birds of the air, and He also takes care of our needs (Matthew 6: 25-27). If the Lord takes care of the birds of the air, how much more important are His children to Him? He not only takes care of all our needs; He also lavishes us with His love (1 John 3:1). He's an extravagant God, a generous God, and a God who goes above and beyond for us. He likes to surprise us, bless us, and give us abundance so that we cannot only receive enough for ourselves, but also have enough to share with the world around us.

Maybe it's time to understand just how the Lord works. He doesn't hold things back from His children. He wants to give us everything. We simply need to learn how to position ourselves to receive from Him. Once Susie and I learned how to position ourselves to receive from Him, as a ministry, we began to see how He continually provides above and beyond our expectations. The Lord wants this for you as well. He wants to equip you with all the resources you require in order to fulfill the commission on your life.

PRAYER

Father,

Thank You that You promise to meet all my needs according to Your riches in glory. Thank You that You care about even the smallest details of my life, and You wish to give me everything I need to live a life glorifying to You. I position and posture myself today in a place of receiving from You. I am grateful for what I have. I will seek first the kingdom of God and believe that all else will be added unto me. Thank You for meeting all my needs. Today, I receive from You, for You are a good Father, and You take care of all my needs. Amen.

The Quest of Abundant Life
REQUIRING RESOURCES

When it comes to resources, what are your needs? List both long-term and short-term needs below.

John says in order to receive from God, we must first learn how to position ourselves to receive. He references one way found in Matthew 6:33. Write the verse below.

When scripture says, "seek first His Kingdom," it is saying we need to make God our priority in life, seeking Him, talking with Him, obeying Him, and walking in His ways. A similar verse is found in Psalm 37:4. Write the verse below.

How are the promises from these two scriptures similar? Each of these promises are conditional, though God's love is unconditional. With each of these scriptures, an action of faith is required on our part. We must seek Him, and we must delight in Him. When we make Him our priority, we humble ourselves before Him, with palms and heart uplifted, releasing our plans and desires, and adopting His plans and desires for our life. Then, we are positioned before Him, ready and able to receive the blessings He releases. What holds you back from positioning yourself to receive from God?

You will find wisdom for your long-term and short-term needs by working through the questions in today's quest. God's Word always brings wisdom for today and tomorrow. Read the prayer from Proverbs 30:7-9 to keep your eyes focused on God and the wealth and wisdom of His provision. Remember, God's provision is always right on time.

PART TWO

ENCOURAGING LIFE

"For I know the plans I have for you," declares the Lord, "plans to prosper you and not to harm you, plans to give you hope and a future."
Jeremiah 29:11

DAY 10

Empowered to Choose

"For you are a people holy to the Lord your God. The Lord your God has chosen you out of all the peoples on the face of the earth to be his people, his treasured possession."
Deuteronomy 7:6

Knowing that we are His chosen people (and that He first chose us) helps us understand that He has empowered us to choose, to make choices. By His death on the cross and His resurrection, Jesus handed back to humanity the power of the Lord. He did this through the forgiveness of our sins and the access to eternal life on earth as it is in heaven.

The Word of God and the power of His Holy Spirit leads us to make choices honoring to the Father, because He loves us so much. His love leads us to make choices and live in ways that are honoring to Him, every step of the way.

Maybe you desire to make better choices. Maybe you are living with the despair and consequences of bad choices made in the past. Today is the day to remember that Jesus has empowered you to choose, because He first chose you. Not because of your works, but because of love.

Think of a situation or circumstance you are in right now. Remind yourself that you have been empowered to choose the way you perceive the situation and to also change your perspective on that situation. You have been empowered to choose how you will respond or react to this difficult situation.

The power of being able to choose means we are no longer led by our thoughts, feelings and emotions. Instead, we are led by the power of the Holy Spirit and the truth of His words.

PRAYER

Lord Jesus,

Thank You that You first chose us and that You made a choice to leave the heavenly realm to come to earth to save us of our sins. You died on the cross to forgive us for our sins that we might have eternal life. Thank You that, on the cross, we were given back the power to make choices. Today I surrender to You, I declare and decree that I wish to make healthy and positive choices that are honoring to You because of my love for You and all that You did for me.

Forgive me for making choices in the past that did not include or involve You. I commit today to place You at the center of all future decisions because of Your love for me. In the mighty name of Jesus, Amen.

The Quest of Abundant Life
· · · · · · · · · · · · ·
EMPOWERED TO CHOOSE

The first and greatest choice in our spiritual walk is the choice to follow Jesus Christ as Lord and Savior. Have you made your choice? Scripture says either we follow Christ, or we follow Satan. There is no middle ground. Choose this day whom you will serve.

In Deuteronomy 31:19-20, Moses says to the Israelites, "Now choose life so that you and your children may live and that you may love the Lord your God, listen to his voice, and hold fast to him. For the Lord is your life." Both in the Old and New Testaments, we see that the abundant life is found by choosing the Lord. In this verse, we see that a part of that choice includes listening to His voice. Have you tuned your spirit to hear the voice of the Lord when He speaks, prompts, or reveals Himself to you? If not, ask Him to open your spiritual eyes and ears so you may see and hear Him.

Read John 8:47. If you belong to God, what are you able to do?

Learning to discern God's voice often seems insurmountable to new believers. In Jeremiah 29:13-14, the Lord declares, "You will seek me and find me when you seek me with all your heart. I will be found by you." To seek something requires effort, research, study, curiosity, and persistence. When you are seeking God, it often requires you to put forth effort by reading scripture, praying, asking questions of Him and waiting for an answer. Don't give up. He promises to show up.

One of the ways we learn to discern God's voice is by walking in obedience to His Word. Not because we are keeping score or following rules, but because we believe that His ways are best and abundant for us and those around us. Read 1 John 5:2-5. Journal the words and phrases from this text that encourage you to walk in obedience to God. Pen a prayer, seeking the help of the Holy Spirit to lead a life of obedience.

DAY 11

· ·

Green Pastures

"The Lord is my shepherd, I shall not be in want.
He makes me lie down in green pastures, he leads
me beside still waters, he restores my soul.
He leads me in the paths of righteousness for His name's sake."
Psalm 23:1-3

The Lord is intentional about restoring life into us. We learn from today's scripture that He *makes* us lie down in green pastures and He leads us beside still waters. You may be asking, "Why does He *make* me lie down in green pastures?"

The Lord knows that our tendency is toward busyness and distraction, taking our eyes off Him at times. Often, He *makes* us lie down in green pastures so we can reconnect with Him and refocus. The quest of receiving abundant life requires us to focus on Jesus alone, to lay down in green pastures, to "be still and know that He is God."

These green pastures are the very training ground where we learn to be still with the Father, to be removed from the distractions life throws at us, and to receive from Him everything that He has for us.

Maybe you have wanted to get into this place of peace and communion with the Father for a long time. Maybe you have desired to be still with the Lord and know more of Him. Today, He is calling you into these green pastures. He's removing distractions from your life. He's calling you to come to Him, one-on-one, so He can inject the abundant life into you by speaking clearly and giving you direction.

PRAYER

Lord God,

Thank You that You make me lie down in green pastures. I confess this is not always easy or natural for me, especially when life is busy. Today, I choose to carve out a space to lie down with You in green pastures, to hear Your voice and to simply rest in Your presence. It is good to simply be and not always do. Today I choose to take a deep breath and a reset with You. Lead me beside still waters, Lord, and restore my soul. In the mighty name of Jesus. Amen.

The Quest of Abundant Life
· · · · · · · · · · · ·
GREEN PASTURES

In 1 Kings 19, we find Elijah, the prophet of God, running in fear for his life. In verse 4, he says, "I have had enough, Lord. Take my life." Then Elijah lay down and slept. What was the Lord's response? He brought Psalm 23 to life for Elijah. Read the account in 1 Kings 19:1-9. How did the Lord minister to Elijah?

In the same account of Elijah, consider that the Lord *made* Elijah rest so that he could be restored. Have there been times in your life when you know the Lord caused circumstances so that you could rest and be restored? Explain.

In today's key verse, the first words are, "The Lord is my shepherd." Make a list of the things a shepherd does while keeping watch over his flock of sheep. Use an internet browser if needed to discover as many responsibilities as possible of how a shepherd tends to their flock.

By meditating on the list above, do you have a clearer image of the way the Lord is your shepherd and how He watches over you? Journal your response to what you have learned through this exercise.

Literally, make time in your schedule to be outdoors and lay in the grass, free from electronics and other distractions. Use your imagination to see the Lord sitting beside you, ministering to your fear, your disappointments, your insecurities, your lack, and your emotional emptiness. As you sit with Him, allow Him into the innermost parts of your being so He can apply His healing balm of love and tenderness to your wounds. In this, He is restoring your soul.

DAY 12

. . . .

Stepping Out

"Immediately Jesus made the disciples get into the boat and go on ahead of him to the other side, while he dismissed the crowd...During the fourth watch of the night Jesus went out to them, walking on the lake. When the disciples saw him walking on the lake, they were terrified. 'It's a ghost,' they said, and cried out in fear. But Jesus immediately said to them: 'Take courage! It is I. Don't be afraid.' 'Lord, if it's you,' Peter replied, 'tell me to come to you on the water.' 'Come,' he said. Then Peter got down out of the boat, walked on the water and came toward Jesus. But when he saw the wind, he was afraid and, beginning to sink, cried out, 'Lord, save me!' Immediately Jesus reached out his hand and caught him."
Matthew 14:22-33

When the disciples were in the middle of the storm, the Lord did not allow them to stay there alone. He went out to them, walking on the lake. Then He called them to step outside of their comfort zone and to walk with Him.

The Lord challenges us to take risks and step out on His behalf. Taking risks and stepping out both involve action and discomfort. Why? Because comfort can be the place where our dreams go to die. To take action says we are not going to stay where we are and declares that we are stepping out in faith, into the plans and purposes the Lord has for us. We often find abundant life in stepping out.

Here's the great part. When we choose to step out of our comfort zone and onto the water with Jesus, there is a promise that we will get to dry land. We learn from Peter that, the moment he stepped out of the boat and onto the water with Jesus, he was safe, hand in hand with Jesus. But the moment he took his eyes off Jesus, he began to cry out, "Lord, save me." The Lord immediately grabbed hold of him and saved him. He led Peter to dry land.

The Lord wants to do the same for you. He challenges you to step out of your comfort zone, to step out of difficult situations and circumstances, and step on the water, hand in hand with Jesus. He promises to lead you to dry land if you take courage and step out with Him onto the water.

PRAYER

Father,

I admit I am comfortable where I am. I want to receive the full abundant life You have for me, and I want to learn what it is to take risks and step out. Thank You for the lessons learned in today's key scripture when Peter recognized You in the middle of the storm and chose to step out onto the waters with You. Today I surrender my life, I surrender my choices, rights, and desires. Today I choose to take the first step onto the water with You. I trust You to lead me safely to dry land. I trust You to lead me into the plans and purposes that You have for my life. Today I am stepping out, not by myself, but hand in hand with You. Amen.

The Quest of Abundant Life
. . . .
STEPPING OUT

The Lord often calls us outside our comfort zone so that we may experience the stretching and sharing of our faith and resources. Ask Him to open your eyes, ears, and spirit to step out in courage and boldness to have the faith to "walk on the water" with Him.

Scripture helps us understand how others took risks and stepped out of their comfort zone in following the Lord. This journey through scripture will help you on your quest:

Genesis 12:1:   What did the Lord ask Abram to do?

Genesis 12:2-3:   What did the Lord promise Abram as his reward for obedience?

Exodus 3:10:   What was God's plan and purpose for Moses?

Exodus 4:13:   What was Moses' initial response?

Exodus 6:4:   Where was God going to send Moses and the Israelites?

Exodus 34:10-12: How did God honor the obedience of Moses?

Matthew 4:19:   When Jesus called Peter to "Come, follow me," what did He tell Peter his new role in life would be? What did Jesus mean by this?

Acts 2:14-21:   How do these verses show how the promise made to Peter in Matthew 4:19 was fulfilled?

By reading the accounts of Abram, Moses, and Peter, how are you encouraged to take a leap of faith and allow the stretching of your faith to occur? Has the Lord asked you to step out of your comfort zone to follow Him, yet you hold back because of fear of failure or rejection?

DAY 13

. . . .

Cultivating Courage

"Therefore, keep up your courage
for I believe God that it will turn out exactly as I have been told."
Acts 27:27

These are the times and seasons where Christians are required to find their voice, to step out in boldness and courage, and believe the Lord will turn things around as He told us. But cultivating courage is a discipline that takes time. As we step out and take risks, our courage grows, develops, and is cultivated.

Many of us are not naturally gifted in the area of courage because we have not learned to trust the Lord. When we trust Him to do what He says He will do, then we rise in courage and take risks, even when it looks like we are facing the impossible. Having courage that things may work out differently than we initially expect means we have more of a chance to see a miraculous outcome.

We see time and again in scripture that when people stepped out, when they placed their courage and trust in the Lord, He delivered them every single time. He wants to deliver you today. He wants to show you amazing things. He wants you to step out, have courage, and believe that He will do what He has promised in His Word.

Maybe you find yourself in the middle of an impossible situation or circumstance right now, and you feel like you are stuck, not knowing how or where to move. Part of receiving the abundant life is believing the Lord and having courage to step out and see that things can change. He is the

God of the impossible, the God who can and does turn things around, when you place your trust and belief in Him.

PRAYER

Lord,

Thank You for challenging me to grow in courage, to place my faith and trust fully in You. Give me courage to step out in the name of Jesus to do the most amazing things. Thank You that the Spirit of the Lord is upon me and inside me, and that I am an ambassador of Christ. I will do more and greater things than even the Lord Jesus Christ. That's a big encouragement. I receive supernatural courage today from the throne room of heaven, and I will activate this courage by stepping out in faith to see the impossible take place, even when I have not seen it before. In the mighty name of Jesus. Amen.

The Quest of Abundant Life
· · · · · · · · · · · ·
CULTIVATING COURAGE

Walking in obedience to Christ not only involves stepping outside our comfort zone and taking risks, it requires that we muster the courage to take the first step. Be reminded: When God speaks a promise into our heart, we are guaranteed the outcome. For confirmation of this statement, read Acts 27:25. Write the verse below.

When God created us, He knew we would constantly and consistently face fear in our lives. Often in scripture He says, "Do not fear." Other times, He encourages us to "be courageous." Courage is the opposite of fear. What situation do you face in life where fear cripples you, but you need courage to rise up?

Fill in the blank below in response to your above answer.

Lord, today I bring before you this situation of _____. The answer and resolution of this seems impossible. Lord, today I declare that I will approach this situation again, but this time, I will approach it with a new level of courage. Give me wisdom and courage to _____ _____. Because I approach this situation with a new level of faith and courage, I know I will see this situation turn itself around. In the mighty name of Jesus. Amen.

Faith and courage go hand in hand. In Matthew 17:20, what does scripture say I can do if I have faith as small as a mustard seed?

In response to the above question, pray this prayer:
Lord, increase my faith. Help me believe in You and Your mighty works. Pair my faith and courage, Lord, so they give me the strength and inspiration to believe that You always do as You have said. Help my unbelief. May I rest in knowing that You will work good from this situation that has me parked in neutral. Infuse me with courage to take steps forward, trusting that You go before me to prepare the way, and You come behind me as my rear guard.

DAY 14

· ·

Finding Your Voice

He said to them, "Go into all the world and
preach the good news to all creation.
Whoever believes and is baptized will be saved, but whoever does not believe
will be condemned. And these signs will accompany those who believe:
In my name they will drive out demons; they will speak in new tongues;
they will pick up snakes with their hands; and
when they drink deadly poison,
it will not hurt them at all; they will place their
hands on sick people, and they will get well."
Mark 16:15-18

If anyone can encourage you in the area of finding your voice, it is me. What a journey it's been from feeling like I was nobody to finally arriving at the place where I found my God-given voice. Even this book is a testimony to God's miraculous power of taking someone who feels inadequate, who does not feel good enough, and who feels they do not have anything good to give and turning it around.

Previously, we have covered the importance of understanding our identity in Christ and recognizing the lies of Satan. Once our identity has been discovered, once God's truth begins to saturate the soul and spirit and become part of our spiritual DNA, we experience the opening of our vocal chords and learn to recognize a new sound – the sound of our God-given voice, wrapped in the authority that comes to us through the Holy Spirit.

Scripture tells us we are called to go into all the world and preach the good news to everybody. Preaching the good news literally means finding our voice, speaking it out, and sharing with others. To be effective Christians, it is imperative that we find our voice and that we share our testimony with others. The more we share, the more the lies of the enemy disappear. Using our voice helps us stand firm in our identity as children of God.

I've had the opportunity of ministering to many people who have felt inadequate and without a voice. It's amazing to see someone set free from the enemy's bondage of trying to steal their voice. Maybe today you feel like that person who has no voice. It's time to find your voice. I declare over you that today your voice is being released in the mighty name of Jesus.

PRAYER

Father God,

Thank You that I have been given a voice. You tell me to go into all the world and preach the good news to everyone. I have learned about the importance of cultivating courage, and today I ask You to give me my voice. Place Your fingers on my pulse and return my voice to me. Speak to my identity and my heart. Reveal to me just how powerful You have made me in Your image, and that You call me to take the gospel to the ends of the earth. Reveal to me that You have created me in Your image. Today I commit to finding my voice, to opening my mouth, and to releasing what You have placed inside me. I trust that, if my words come from You, they will be a blessing and benefit to all those around me. In the mighty name of Jesus. Amen.

The Quest of Abundant Life
. . . .
FINDING YOUR VOICE

A big part of finding our voice is the discovery of learning what and how we believe. Scripture says we are to use our voice to teach, preach, prophecy, declare, and share our knowledge of God with the world. Does the thought of using your voice in this way cause you fear? Read Psalm 81:10. What does the Lord say He will do when we open our mouth to speak for Him?

Let's do a doubletake and see where we can find this same promise in scripture, as it applies to one of God's chosen leaders. Look in Exodus 4:12. In speaking to Moses, what does the Lord say He will do when we open our mouth to speak for Him?

To find our voice, we often need to search. And there's no better place to search for answers than in the scriptures. So once more, what does the Lord say in Luke 12:11-12 He will do when we open our mouth to speak for Him?

In Luke 12:12, when will the Holy Spirit give us words to speak?

When God sends you out to share your story or to speak truth, it's good to plan and prepare what you will say. Not because the Holy Spirit needs your help, but because you want to be a good steward of the opportunities God gives you to share the gospel. However, when you speak on the Lord's behalf, always push aside your thoughts, preparations and plans, and allow the Holy Spirit to speak through you. All of your best-laid plans are nothing and powerless unless they are infused with the power and authority of the Holy Spirit. The reason we find our voice is so we can surrender that same voice to the Holy Spirit so He can speak and move through us. Everything we do is for one purpose. That purpose is explained in 1 Peter 2:12. What is that purpose?

DAY 15

. . . .

Heavenly Places

"And God raised us up with Christ and seated us
with Him in the heavenly realms in Christ Jesus."
Ephesians 2:6

Our position and posture before Christ and before the world are key in the quest of finding abundant life. When we realize that the Lord has seated us with Christ Jesus in heavenly places, we begin to hold our heads differently, we walk upright, we know who we are and who we represent. We may only be earthly beings right now, but we have heavenly callings upon our lives, and we are called to dwell with the King of Kings and Lord of Lords in heavenly places.

In the Lord's prayer found in Matthew 6:9-13, we read, "your Kingdom come, your will be done, on earth as it is in heaven." This means our focus should be on the conditions of the Kingdom of heaven. We should be pulling the Kingdom of heaven down to earth and seeing it manifest wherever we go.

Being a missionary to Colombia, Susie and I often experience the pulling down of God's will and plan from heaven into the earth realm. We understand our identity and calling to sit with Christ in heavenly places and simply be a vessel to pull heaven to earth, not in our own strength but in the strength that Jesus gives to us.

The Lord is reminding you that you have been called by the Father to sit in heavenly places. Take a look at yourself. When people meet you and when they speak to you, would they know from your behavior, speech, and faith in Jesus that you have been called to heavenly places? Wouldn't you love to be willing and able to call others to a higher place in life? In order to do that, you must first get there. The Lord is calling you higher, He's calling you to sit with Him in heavenly places.

Today may your perspective change. May you see the world from a different vantage point and viewpoint. May you be reset and realigned into your position of the heavenly place so you can be more effective and reach more people for Christ. You are an ambassador of Christ, you are more than a conqueror, and you are called to dwell with Christ Jesus in heavenly places.

PRAYER

Lord,

Thank You for Your Word that tells me that God raised me up with Christ and seated me with Him in heavenly places. Right now, in the mighty name of Jesus, I come before the throne room of God, humbly surrendering my life and taking my rightful place with Christ in heavenly places. Thank You that, because I have done that, my perspective will change, and I will do things differently because I now understand the authority given to me because I am seated in heavenly places. Thank You, Lord, for taking away the old things and bringing in the new things. Thank You that things will never be the same again. In the name of Jesus. Amen.

The Quest of Abundant Life
· · · · · · · · · · · ·
HEAVENLY PLACES

Today we are in the quest to understand the heavenly places where we are seated with Christ. Because of the resurrection of Christ, we know that our bodies will one day be raised from the dead. We also know that we have been given the power to live as Christians now. For proof, read Ephesians 1:19-20. Journal any words or phrases that resonate with your spirit.

To understand why Jesus is seated at the right hand of God in the heavenly realm, read Philippians 2:6-11. List what you discover in the space below.

Read Ephesians 1:20-21. List the things that Christ is seated above, as He is seated at the right hand of Father God.

Because scripture says we are seated with Christ in the heavenly realm, we understand this means we, as God's children, are also exposed to the spiritual forces of evil in the heavenly realms and are often called to spiritual battle. We are told in Ephesians 6:10 to be strong in the Lord and in His mighty power. We also know that God is always victorious in every battle He sends us into! Read Ephesians 6:10-19. In the space below, draw a stick figure. As you read through scripture, dress the figure in the armor of God.

In your drawing, beside each piece of armor, write what the armor represents.

DAY 16

. . . .

Authority and Influence

"I tell you the truth, anyone who has faith in
me will do what I have been doing.
He will do even greater things than these, because I am going to the Father.
And I will do whatever you ask in my name, so that
the Son may bring glory to the Father.
You may ask me for anything in my name, and I will do it."
John 14:12-14

As we increase in our knowledge of who we are and what we are called to do, and as we increase in the security of our identity in Christ, the Word says that we may ask for anything in His name, knowing that the Father will be glorified, and He will do it. That is the perfect example of authority.

Authority and influence are directly linked. As we grow in our level of authority, the circles of people in which we influence become larger, and the way we influence people becomes more effective.

In Matthew 28:18, Jesus said, "All authority in heaven and on earth has been given to me." When Jesus ascended into heaven, He sent His Holy Spirit to earth, and delegated His authority to those who call themselves sons and daughter of the Father.

In the Great Commission found in Matthew 28:18-19, Jesus said, "All authority in heaven and on earth has been given to me. Therefore, go and make disciples of all nations, baptizing them in the name of the Father and of the Son and of the Holy Spirit, and teaching them to obey everything I have commanded you."

When Jesus ascended into heaven, He sent His Holy Spirit to earth, and delegated His authority to those He calls sons and daughters. The Great Commission says, "go and make disciples." This is a great example of authority which, in turn, leads to greater influence.

PRAYER

Lord Jesus,

Thank You for the authority You delegated to me upon leaving this earth and returning to the Father. Your Word tells me that I shall do even greater things than You did while on this earth. I receive Kingdom authority today. I choose to say yes to the Great Commission, to go into all nations, making disciples, baptizing them in the name of the Father, the Son, and the Holy Spirit, and to teach them to obey everything You have commanded. I receive today all authority which leads to greater influence. In the mighty name of Jesus. Amen.

The Quest of Abundant Life
············
AUTHORITY AND INFLUENCE

Read Genesis 1:26-30. In this passage, the Lord gave man authority over all the earth. List the things the Lord put under the authority of man.

In Genesis 3 we read about the fall of man and how sin separated him from God. In choosing to obey the snake (Satan) rather than God, man handed his authority over the earth to Satan. In verses 14-19, notice the consequences this choice brought to Satan, to man, and to woman. List them below.

Hebrews 5:8 says of Jesus, "Although He was a son, He learned obedience from what He suffered." Jesus chose to obey the Father, even to death. It is through His obedience that our authority in the earth has been restored. Read Philippians 2:6-11. In verses 9-11, how did God honor the obedience of Christ?

In Matthew 28:18, Jesus commissions His followers with authority and power. What does He tell us to do? Where does He tell us to go?

The life of Jesus has influenced the world in amazing ways. Your life, surrendered to Christ, will change the world in ways you cannot even imagine. You have more influence than you can possibly realize when you use it for the glory of God and the good of mankind. "The world has yet to see what God will do with a man fully consecrated to Him." -Dwight Lyman Moody. Pen a prayer below, inviting the Holy Spirit to teach you how to have a greater influence and authority in the earth.

. . . .

Kingdom Ambassador

"We are therefore Christ's ambassadors, as though
God were making his appeal through us.
We implore you on Christ's behalf: Be reconciled to God."
2 Corinthians 5:20

The dictionary defines the word, "ambassador," as an accredited diplomat sent by a country as its official representative to a foreign country.

Did you know that we are Kingdom ambassadors for Christ? We are the ones who are called to represent Christ in a foreign land.

Christ is seated at the right hand of the Father in heaven, and we are to be His official legal representatives on earth. We speak on behalf of the Father. We do not speak our own words, but we speak the words of the Father. Just like Jesus did. Jesus was the ambassador of the Father and only did what He saw the Father doing, and He only spoke what He heard the Father saying.

My questions to you are, "How well do you feel you represent Jesus? How well do you feel you represent the Father?" I'm sure you can think about many family members or friends who do not know Jesus. Are you doing your best to represent Him to them? Is this an area of life in which you wish to grow?

In order to step closer to the abundant life, I encourage you to dive deeper into being a Kingdom ambassador. As you grow closer to looking more like Christ, you will become more effective at representing Him on earth. As you represent Him well, and as you see those around you respond to Jesus in you, you will receive life, and life in abundance.

There's nothing more satisfying than having people identify and respond to Jesus inside of you. This can only take place when you are a Kingdom ambassador.

PRAYER

Lord,

I recognize that my life is not my own, I recognize that I died to myself when I received Jesus and was empowered by the Holy Spirit. I want to become even more effective as a Kingdom ambassador on earth. May my life reflect Jesus and demonstrate His character and His way of doing things while here on earth. Today, I declare and decree that I am a Kingdom ambassador, and I choose to follow the cloud of Your presence by day and the fire of Your presence by night, into the plans and purposes You have for me, regardless of how difficult and challenging they may be. In the mighty name of Jesus. Amen.

The Quest of Abundant Life
. . . .
KINGDOM AMBASSADOR

How well do you feel you represent Jesus on earth? How well do you feel you represent the Father on earth? Are you doing your best to represent them to your family members and friends?

This is an area of life where we can always improve. Scripture says we are to shine our light for Jesus, to reflect Him, and to make Him known. This requires not only an understanding of God's Word and His ways, but also the maturity that comes by putting this understanding into action. What areas in your life can you can be a greater reflection of Christ?

For a further understanding of being a Kingdom ambassador, look up these scriptures as referenced by John in today's devotional:

John 5:16-19

John 12:49-50

John 14:31

Luke 12:11

The Lord provides wisdom to enable us to be His ambassadors. Read Proverbs chapter 2 and 3 and jot down some of the moral benefits in following His wisdom.

The book of Proverbs is filled with spiritual and practical guidelines in how to live a life that represents Christ. For example, find these scriptures and write the practical wisdom given:

Proverbs 10:12

Proverbs 11:2

Proverbs 14:30

Proverbs 26:20

DAY 18

. . . .

Welcoming Risk

"For I know the plans I have for you," says the Lord. "They are plans
for good and not for disaster to give you a future and a hope."
Jeremiah 29:11

When we know and believe that the Lord has plans for us that are for good
and not for disaster, this should encourage us to take more risks.

We find that stereotypically there are two types of people in society. Those
who are risk takers and those who are risk avoiders. It is easy to note that
those who are risk takers often make more mistakes, learn from them, and
get ahead more quickly.

Risk avoiders tend to hang back and often miss the opportunities laid
before them. They focus more on the risks than the possible positive outcomes they could achieve if the risk were taken in the first place.

Today, challenge yourself to take more risks, even small ones. Perhaps
these are risks you would not have taken before reading this scripture.
Remember, the Lord's plans for you are good, they involve a future and a
hope for your life. They involve stepping out into all that He has for you.
He promises that His plans are not for disaster, but they are for your good.
You cannot fully embrace the abundant life with the Lord if you do not
step out onto the water with Him.

The fear of risk is an area of life many of us try to conquer. There are many
materials in the secular world about overcoming fear and taking risks.
Most importantly, we have the Lord Jesus who walks alongside us, declaring He has good plans for us. As Christians, we have a safety net – even

when we take risks and things do not turn out good, we still know that God is good, and His future hope for us is not for disaster, but is secured in Jesus.

Maybe you have taken risks before and things did not turn out the way you hoped. Or maybe you have taken risks and lost everything. Don't give up. Scripture encourages you to try again, to give it another go. Step up, step out, and risk again. There may be an amazing breakthrough on the other side and you don't want to miss it.

PRAYER

Father,

Thank You that there is a plan and hope for my life. Your plan for my life is good. You will not lead me to disaster, but You lead me into a hope and a future. Help and encourage me to take more risks. Help me to fix my eyes upon You, to step out and see You prosper my life and work things together for good. Thank You, Father, that I no longer choose to avoid risk and hold back, but I choose to push into the things You have for me. In the mighty name of Jesus. Amen.

The Quest of Abundant Life
. . . .
WELCOMING RISK

Take a risk inventory assessment. Do you lean more toward being a risk taker or a risk avoider? If you have taken risks in the past, list a few of the risks that have worked for your good. List a risk that has not turned out as you hoped. How did the outcome of both risks help you grow?

The Lord has a purpose and plan for each life. In Jeremiah 1:5, the Lord basically says, "I knew you, formed you, and fashioned you before you were placed in the womb of your mother. Your life has value, your life has a purpose. Lean into me and I will lead you on your path of destiny." How does that statement fuel your desire to step into the risk of following Christ to achieve His plan for you?

The Bible is filled with people who were risk takers and who experienced the deliverance of the Lord when they stepped out in obedience. Read Daniel 6:6-27. How did Daniel's risk-taking benefit him and God's Kingdom? How did Daniel's risk-taking teach him more about God?

The Bible is also filled us people who wanted confirmation from God before taking a risk. Read Judges 6:36-40. Gideon was a risk avoider but wanted to become a risk taker. What does this scripture teach you about stepping out in faith and obedience as God leads?

If you are a risk avoider, how does the scripture from Jeremiah 29:11 encourage you to step out in faith and trust God to work His plans through your obedience?

DAY 19

. . . .

Perfect Protection

"He will cover you with his feathers and under his wings you will find refuge.
His faithfulness will be your shield and rampart."
Psalm 91:4

It is awesome to know that God is not only our Father, but He is also our protector. Just like any good father, He takes care of His children. How many parents do you know who would actively allow their children to be in harms way? The Lord is just like a good father – He cares for His children and provides for their protection every step of the way.

We recently learned about stepping out and taking risks for Jesus. It is comforting to know that when we step out and risk it all for Christ, He always provides us with protection.

Being on the mission field and being called to dangerous places, Susie and I have experienced the protection of God. When we have been in difficult and challenging situations, we have seen the hand of God move and change our circumstances in order to protect us.

If we are called according to His purposes, and if we are obedient to His will and direction in our lives, no matter how big the risk, no matter how dangerous the situation or circumstances we might find ourselves in, we can remember that He is always our protector. He is the Lord who loves and protects us.

Now is the time for you to start listening carefully to the voice of God. Get intimate and draw near to Him. It is time to crawl under the feather of His wings where you will find refuge and strength. He is the one who challenges you to get out of your comfort zone. He is the one who challenges you to go to the ends of the earth to share His love with others. He promises to protect you every step of the way as you walk in obedience.

Today I want you to know this deep within your heart. When you walk in obedience, you are not at risk, you are not in danger, and you are not alone. You are protected by the mighty hand of God – the God who takes interest in the smaller, finer details of your life.

PRAYER

Lord,

I confess that I do not always feel protected. There are moments in life when it seems I am on my own, hung out to dry without any support or backing. Today I declare and decree that You are my protector. Because I understand that truth, I choose to take risks, to step out and overcome obstacles because I know that You are always by my side, protecting me every single step of the way. In the mighty name of Jesus. Amen.

The Quest of Abundant Life
. . . .
PERFECT PROTECTION

Have there been times in your life when you felt unprotected or that your safety was at risk? Briefly describe below.

Hindsight often helps us see things from a different perspective. God promises to always be with us and to protect us. Spend time remembering the situation from the above question. Where do you see Jesus in that event or situation? How was He your helper and protector?

Read Psalm 121. How does the Lord provide protection over your life and your loved ones? List some of the ways below.

Often God surrounds us with heavenly angels to provide our protection. Read 2 Kings 6:16-17 for an example of how God's angelic provision protected Elisha and his servant. Pray verse 17 over your situation and circumstances. Journal that prayer below.

Meditate on this truth today. When fear tries to grasp you and hold you back, remember you are protected in both the spiritual and earthly realm by God's mighty hand. For more scripture about God's protection, read: Psalm 23:1, Isaiah 43:1-2, and John 10:27-28.

DAY 20

. . . .

Guaranteed Good

"And we know that in all things God works
for the good of those who love him,
who have been called according to his purpose."
Romans 8:28

By simply reading and applying scripture to our lives, we have access to the abundant life. Romans 8:28 is a guarantee that characterizes our lives as Christians. We have a God who works all things together for good for those who love Him and have been called according to His purpose.

Four questions to consider are: How much do you love the Lord? How much do you devote your time to Him? How much do you fix your eyes upon Him? How often do you declare your love for Him?

Think about a seemingly impossible situation or circumstance in your life. Speak these words over it, "Because I love and follow Him, God is turning this situation around. He is moving mountains. He is doing the impossible because He is working this out, to use it for my good and for His glory."

Choose to believe that His promises are true. Choose to believe that your situation or circumstance does not have to remain the same, and it can be used for good. Understand that oftentimes, we do not see the good workings of God in the moment, but in hindsight we see how God used impossible situations to push us forward, to teach and grow us in His likeness, and to bring glory to His name.

The Lord says what the enemy means for evil, He turns for good (Genesis 50:20). The Lord wants to show the enemy who is the strongest force. He wants to show the enemy that He is victorious. I decree and declare victory over your situation, that the Lord is turning things around for good. Trust God to work everything out for good. As you declare this with your mouth and believe this in your heart, you will see a miraculous turnaround in your situation. In the mighty name of Jesus.

PRAYER

Father,

I declare my love for You. I declare that I am in awe of You. I glorify Your name. I magnify You and I fix my eyes upon You and You alone. Open my eyes to see Your activity in this situation. Help me trust You more. I believe that You are turning things around for good. What the enemy meant for evil You are using for good. You are turning this situation around and I will see a measurable difference in the future. Thank You, Father, in the mighty name of Jesus. Amen.

The Quest of Abundant Life

· · · · · · · · · · · ·

GUARANTEED GOOD

Do you love the Lord? Scripture says we are to love Him with all our heart, soul, body and strength. That means with every ounce of our being. Can you say that you love Him in this way? Loving God in this way is a giant step into abundant life, life and more life.

How much time do you devote to Him? Not to fulfill a religious checklist, but to engage with Him, to build a relationship with Him, to talk to Him. A formal appointment does not need to be made to meet with Him. You can talk with Him as you walk along the road, as you sit in your car, as you go about your chores. He is closer to you than your next breath. How much time do you devote to getting to know Him and being known by Him?

How often do you fix your eyes upon Him and declare your love for Him? To fix your eyes upon Him is to see Him in all of life's circumstances and situations, to see life through His gaze and His perspective. Abundant life is multiplied when everyday life and troubles are seen through the inner workings of God.

Ask God to give you His vision so you can see things from His perspective. When this happens, you can see how He works the seemingly impossible situations to bring glory to His name and to bring good out of perceived bad. With this supernatural vision, everything in life begins to make more sense.

What is the situation or circumstance in your life that needs to be turned from impossible or bad to good? Briefly describe it below, then apply Romans 8:28 to it by writing the scripture beside the situation.

PART THREE

ABUNDANT LIFE

"I have come that they may have life and have it to the full."
John 10:10

"Welcome to the abundant life. Life, life and more life.
Nothing missing, nothing lacking, nothing broken."
John Bell

DAY 21

Exciting Eternity

"Your Kingdom come, your will be done on earth as it is in heaven."
Matthew 6:10

We've already learned that we are called to be ambassadors of Christ and that we do things in His strength and not in our own strength. We do not represent ourselves, but we represent the King of Kings and Lord of Lords on this earth. There's a process involved in walking in His strength and representing Him. That process is in dying to self, which allows Jesus to fully move inside of us.

As we think further about our exciting eternity, it is important to realize and notice that we can live in a heaven-on-earth state today. We are not waiting for the moment we are promoted to glory. We don't just go from this earthly place to a heavenly place, but we can, in fact, live in a heaven-like state while on earth.

Our key scripture says, "Your Kingdom come, your will be done, on earth as it is in heaven." This means we are called as ambassadors of Christ to pull heaven to earth. We are to be assured of our salvation and of our eternal life which was given freely on the cross when Jesus died, was buried, and rose again. When we were forgiven of our sins, when we repented and turned from our wicked ways, we were not only healed, delivered, and set free but we were given access to eternity, even now.

This is so exciting and encouraging. Why not start living with this true reality right now. This will transform how we live and to what level we live. The abundant life is about living life to the full. Life, life, and more life. Nothing missing, nothing lacking, and nothing broken. We can have access to that very life right here, right now.

PRAYER

Lord,

I am not satisfied with the life I am living right now. I learn in scripture that I can have access to a heaven-on-earth state right here, right now, because of the works of the Cross and all Jesus did for me. Help me, Lord, to be a chief encourager, an agent of change, and to instill a heaven-on-earth state to all those around me. Thank You that I do not have to wait until the day I die to enjoy the promise of an exciting eternity. I can choose to begin living it right now. Today I receive the encouragement, the excitement, and the promise of my future in eternity. In the name of Jesus. Amen.

The Quest of Abundant Life
. . . .
EXCITING ETERNITY

Read John 3:16. What does this scripture tell us about eternal life?

In John 3:30, John the Baptist expresses a desire that should resonate with the hearts of all believers. What does he say?

Today's devotional mentions the process of dying to self which allows Jesus to move more fully inside of us. In 1 Corinthians 2:12, we learn that we, as believers, have received the Holy Spirit, which is from God. Read 2 Corinthians 5:14-15. Who are we to live for and why?

The above verse from 2 Corinthians 5 helps us see that we are a new cre-ation, filled with eternal life at the moment of salvation. Turn to Galatians 2:20 and be reminded who lives within you and empowers you to walk out eternity in the here and now.

How do you live in light of eternity while on earth? By allowing the Holy Spirit to become more and selfish desires to become less. By following Christ through obeying His words. Read 1 Peter 4:7-11 for spiritual direction in how to live today in fullness and abundance.

DAY 22

· ·

Cloud Coverage

"The Lord was going before them in a pillar of cloud by day to lead
them on the way and in a pillar of fire by night to give them light that
they might travel by day and by night. He did not take away the pillar
of cloud by day nor the pillar of fire by night from before the people."
Exodus 13:21-22

We've been journeying toward abundant life, life and more life. Nothing missing, nothing lacking, and nothing broken, walking into our future and receiving everything the good Father wants to give us.

We know that life is a journey. It's not always about the final destination, but rather, it's about finding enjoyment and life in the journey itself.

In Exodus 13, we see that we never journey alone. The Lord traveled with the Israelites, providing His guidance, His covering, and His protection. In the daytime, His presence was seen in the form of a pillar of cloud. In the nighttime, His presence was seen in the form of a pillar of fire.

Did you know that the Lord, just as He did with the Israelites, is leading, guiding, and protecting us every step of the way? Knowing that we are protected, that we have the Lord walking with us, should bring us comfort. We are never alone. We do not face the situations and circumstances of this life by ourselves. The Lord Himself is with us.

Know that if you are feeling alone, like you cannot do it, there is a pillar of cloud (the Holy Spirit) leading you. It's ahead of you, it knows what is next. All we need to do is trust in the Lord's leading. If we follow the pillar of cloud by day and the pillar of fire by night, He will deliver us. He will lead us to dry land. He will lead us out of captivity and into the promised land. That is His Word, and His Word is true.

We see in Exodus 13 that the pillars of fire and cloud were never removed from before the people until they reached their destination. Rest assured that the Lord is always behind, beside, and ahead of you, leading, protecting, and guiding you.

PRAYER

Lord,

Today we thank You and acknowledge that You are our pillar of cloud by day and our pillar of fire by night. We want to be obedient to Your will over our lives. We commit ourselves into Your hands declaring that we will follow wherever You lead. Help us recognize and identify Your pillar of cloud by day and Your pillar of fire by night. Help us remain obedient no matter how challenging or difficult it may seem because we know You will deliver us. Thank You that You never leave us nor forsake us. You are always ahead of us and always lead us into safe places and onto dry land. In the mighty name of Jesus. Amen.

The Quest of Abundant Life
· · · · · · · · · · · ·
CLOUD COVERAGE

Read Isaiah 52:12. How does the Lord accompany you when you walk in obedience?

"Do not be afraid of man, for I am with you and will rescue you, declares the Lord." Jeremiah 1:8. Look up the meaning of the word "declare." Write the meaning. How does this word boldly guarantee this promise?

In scripture the clouds often represent the presence of God. (See Psalm 78:14 and Daniel 7:2). Make space in your week to observe the move-ment of the clouds in the sky. Observe how the cloud coverage provides protection from the sun and accompanies a storm by bringing rain. Even through the clouds, God provides protection and provision. What else did you observe?

God also guides and protects us with the prompting of His Holy Spirit. Read John 10:2-4. How does the shepherd lead His sheep?

Read John 10:27. Are you a listener? Does this verse echo in your heart that you need to draw near to the shepherd so you can hear His voice? If you do not hear from Him, how can you follow?

DAY 23

Angelic Assistance

"If you say the Lord is my refuge and you make the Most High your dwelling, no harm will overtake you, no disaster will come near your tent, for He will command his angels concerning you, to guard you in all your ways. They will lift you up in their hands so you will not strike your foot against the stone. You will tread on the lion and cobra; you will trample the great lion and the serpent."
Psalm 91:9-13

This is an extremely encouraging scripture. We learn that the Lord is our refuge and He is the place where we can dwell in safety. We learn that no harm will overtake us, and no disaster will come near our families when we choose to rest in the dwelling place of the Most High and believe that He is our refuge. And we learn that we have angels assisting us every step of the way on this journey of following the Lord.

As we see in 2 Kings 6:17, the Lord often comes to our aid by sending angels to do His bidding and His work. We are told in Hebrews 1:14 that the angels are ministering spirits, sent by God to serve those who have received salvation through Jesus Christ. Often when we cry for help, God sends His angels to lift us in their hands so that we will not strike our foot against the stone. The angels bring protection and they bring angelic covering. They protect us on the Lord's behalf and they also encourage us in the abundant life the Lord has laid before us.

We are wise to understand the role of the angels which is to obey the Father. In scripture, we see that the angels worship God both day and night; they minister to and help God's children, and they deliver messages as sent by God. But they are not worthy of our worship and we do not pray to angels. God alone deserves our worship, praise, and petitions in prayer. Today I encourage you to lift your eyes to the realm of the supernatural to acknowledge the presence of angels.

PRAYER

Father,

I recognize that You have commanded angels to stand with me on this journey of life. Open my eyes to see the protection and provision You send me through the angelic hosts. Thank You for commanding angels to guard me in all my ways. Knowing that I have the host of angel armies surrounding me, protecting me from harm, and encouraging me to step out and live the abundant life brings me great comfort. I acknowledge that You are the commander of all angelic forces. Help me, Lord, to give You the situations and circumstances that I face and the hardships of my life, trusting that You command angels to assist me and war on my behalf. In the mighty name of Jesus. Amen.

The Quest of Abundant Life
· · · · · · · · · · · · ·
ANGELIC ASSISTANCE

What do we know about angels? Journal your answer after both scripture references below.

Psalm 103:20-21

2 Peter 2:11

How do angels carry out God's plan on earth? Journal your answer to the scripture references below.

2 Samuel 24:16-17

Daniel 10:13

Zechariah 1:10-11

Matthew 16:27

Luke 1:11-19

Luke 15:10

As intriguing and wonderful as angels are, they are also God's creation and they move in accordance with the commands of God. We are not to worship angels. Rather, we are to join them in worship of God, the one who is Holy. For further explanation, read:

Colossians 2:18

Revelation 19:10

DAY 24

. . . .

Supernatural Strength

"He gives strength to the weary and increases the power of the weak.
Even young men stumble and fall but those who hope in the Lord
will renew their strength. They will soar on wings like eagles, they
will run and not grow weary, they will walk and not faint."
Isaiah 40:29-31

Is this your cry? "Lord, I am tired and weary. Father, the reality is that at times, I feel as if I cannot go on, as if this journey is too hard, as if the abundant life is for others but not for me."

In Isaiah 40, we see that the Lord focuses on those who are weary and tired. We see that He is interested in those who do not have the energy and life that the Bible encourages and offers to us. God is compassionate and loving, and He chooses to give strength to the weary and increase the power of the weak.

Today the Lord wants to impart supernatural strength to you, to give you everything you need in this time and in this season to achieve all that He has called you to achieve. Think about the situation that has made you tired, has taken your strength and energy, and give it to the Lord. His shoulders are broad and wide. He wants to take your worries and concerns and in return, give you strength and hope.

Those who hope in the Lord will renew their strength. He wants you to soar on wings like eagles, to change your perspective from earthly things as you fix your eyes upon things that are supernatural.

You will run and not grow weary; you will walk and not faint. Receive the strength of the Lord today. He is your refuge and your strength. He is your defender. He is the one who cares for you. His grace is sufficient for you and His power is made perfect in your weakness.

PRAYER

Lord,

I surrender all. I surrender my failures, fears, and fatigue. I am weary, but You give me strength. Thank You, Lord, that when I am weary, You are stronger. Though my flesh may fail, Your spirit is strong in me. I receive Your spirit today, Lord, that empowers me to have hope and empowers me to soar on wings like eagles. I decree and declare that I will run and not grow weary. I decree and declare that I will walk and not be faint. Lord, I also ask that You pour out your strength on my weary family and friends. I intercede on their behalf and ask that You pour out supernatural strength on them. Amen.

The Quest of Abundant Life
. . . .
SUPERNATURAL STRENGTH

Read 2 Corinthians 12:7-10. How do these verses assure you that your weakness is to God's gain?

Hebrews 11 is known as the "Hall of Fame" for heroes of faith. In Hebrews 11:7, how did Noah demonstrate faith and strength in the face of man's ridicule and condemnation? For a further account of Noah and his call to build an ark, read Genesis 6-8.

In Hebrews 11:23-29, we read about Moses. God gave him supernatural faith and strength to rescue the Israelites from Egypt. What does verse 26 say was the reason God infused Moses with supernatural strength?

When God leads us to take a risk or to walk in obedience, He gives us the faith and strength to carry out what He has called us to do. Often, we fall back in fear, afraid He will not be faithful in supplying all our needs. Read Philippians 4:19. Which needs does God promise to supply when we walk in obedience to Him?

Remember this. God gives supernatural strength to the weary and He gives supernatural power to the weak as we walk out His plans and destiny for our life. Don't be held back by fear but step forward in faith and He will meet you where you are, with an abundance of strength, power, and faith.

DAY 25

Prophetic Power

"So we have the prophetic word made more sure, to which you do
well to pay attention, as to a lamp shining in a dark place until
the day dawns and the morning star arises in your hearts."
2 Peter 1:19

The area of prophecy and the prophetic are popular topics in the body of Christ. Those who are called to the office of prophet use words and revelations that enable and empower us to step into our destiny and into our true identity, which is imperative. It seems everyone desires to receive a prophetic word from a known prophet or to receive clarity on our future and how to move forward through supernatural information. The prophetic should inform us of who we are and how to live that out. The reason for desiring the prophetic should always be to advance the Kingdom of God and to live the full complete life that the Father has for us.

Not everyone is called to the office of prophet, as explained in Ephesians 4:11. But we are all called to prophesy, to speak the wisdom and revelations the Lord places within us that bring encouragement and understanding to others.

As believers, we do not need to seek out a well-known prophet to receive direction from God. We are equipped to hear the Lord's voice, personally and intimately, and spirit to spirit. His Word reminds us that He is spirit, and we worship and know Him from within our spirit; we relate spirit to spirit.

God's voice is like a lamp that shines a light in dark places, giving us clarity and direction. The prophetic becomes clear in our lives as we grow confident in hearing God's voice for ourselves and for those around us. We see that we achieve more of what He has for us. We are able to activate what we see in order to become more efficient and effective on behalf of the Kingdom.

Today is a day to listen to His heartbeat, to draw closer to the Father, and to ask for wisdom, strategy, and details on moving forward from where we are to where He wants us to be.

PRAYER

Father,

Thank You for the spirit of prophecy and that You speak to Your children clearly. When we hear Your voice, we recognize You and know You. Lord, help us be obedient to the things You say to us, to the challenges You place before us, and to receive and activate the prophetic in this season. Thank You that as we journey into the abundant life, life and more life, the prophetic will grow, and we will begin to hear You more clearly and become more obedient in following You. In the mighty name of Jesus. Amen

The Quest of Abundant Life
· · · · · · · · · · · ·
PROPHETIC POWER

Read 2 Peter 1:20-21. Where does prophecy have its origin?

Amos 3:7 says, "Surely the Sovereign Lord does nothing without revealing His plan to His servants the prophets." Why does God foretell us what He plans beforehand?

In John 15:15, we are called "friends of Jesus." Why does Jesus say we are called "friends" rather than "servants?"

Look up and write the definition of the word, "prophesy." To prophesy is to speak as directed by God. In Ezekiel 37:4, what did the Lord tell Ezekiel to do? What happened in verses 7-8?

In his devotional, John said, "Not all are called to the office of prophet, but we are all called to prophesy," so speak truth as the Lord leads. Read 1 Corinthians 14:3-5. What is the purpose of the gift of prophecy? Ask the Holy Spirit to open your understanding and to fill you with this gift.

DAY 26

· ·

Precise Provision

*"Seek ye first the Kingdom of God and His righteousness,
and all else will be added unto you."*
Matthew 6:33

Sometimes in the body of Christ, we focus on our needs. We get stuck asking the Lord for things that we want and need instead of seeking His face and seeking Him first, knowing that everything else will be given to us. The challenge is to sincerely seek His face by making Him the priority of our lives. Not because of what we can receive, but purely for the purpose of knowing Him.

Psalm 37:4 reminds us that when we delight ourselves in the Lord, He will give us the desires of our heart. Again, we are told that the Lord is to be the priority of our lives. When this happens, our wants and needs fall by the wayside because we learn that if we want or need something, the good Father will provide for our needs, exactly, precisely, and always. It is imperative that we know Him more fully so that we move further into the abundant life, life and more life where there's nothing missing, nothing lacking, and nothing broken.

Maybe you have needs right now, maybe there are situations and circumstances surrounding you involving lack. The encouragement today is to draw close to Jesus, fix your eyes upon Him, seek Him first and rest assured that, if you seek Him first, all else will be added unto you.

Psalm 34:10 says "Those who seek the Lord lack no good thing." That means that you will lack nothing that is good for you. Sometimes we ask for things that are not good for us. Sometimes we ask for things we do not need or require. The key is to hear the Lord's voice and feel His heartbeat, so we know what we need. Then we can present those needs to Him and receive them.

As a missionary family, we often have needs and requirements of resources to serve our people. The Lord has always been faithful to provide for us and for our mission field. He will be faithful to provide for you and your family in this season. Seek Him first and you will lack no good thing. The Lord wants to provide for your every need. It's a matter of positioning and posturing yourself to receive from the Lord. The way to do that is by getting to know Him and seeking Him first

PRAYER

Father,

We position ourselves before You, we fix our eyes upon You, and we take our eyes off our needs, distractions, and lack that surround us. We position ourselves to receive from You and we do that by seeking You wholeheartedly, with every fiber of our being. We declare our love for You and thank You that You are a good father. Thank You for providing for all my needs. Thank You that You are precise in the way You provide. In the mighty name of Jesus. Amen.

The Quest of Abundant Life
....
PRECISE PROVISION

What happens when we draw near or come near to God, as explained in James 4:8?

What happens when we call out to God, whether for guidance, wisdom, help, rescue, protection, or provision, as taught in Jeremiah 33:3?

What do Isaiah 55:6 and Jeremiah 29:12-14 tell us happens when we search for God?

From the scriptures above, we know that God waits for us to turn our face toward Him. When we do, He is ready, willing, and delighted to make Himself known to us. Look at Hebrews 12:2. What happens when you fix your eyes on a goal – whether an earthly or spiritual goal?

We work toward the goals we set our eyes and mind on. When we draw near to God, call on Him and listen with obedient hearts to His Words, our thought processes have an opportunity to be purified and made new.

The Holy Spirit and the Word of God are His provision for helping us renew our mind. Look at Philippians 4:8. How does this scripture teach us to refocus our mind? Can you incorporate this new goal into your daily routine and begin changing your mindset?

DAY 27

. . . .

Lavish Love

*"Above all, love each other deeply because love
covers over a multitude of sins."*
1 Peter 4:8

One of the keys to living the abundant life is learning how to love and how to be loved. This is a two-way process.

First, we learn how our Father's love changes us from the inside out. The fact that His love is unconditional and there is nothing we can do to make Him love us any more is the driving factor that enables us to love those around us. As we read in the key scripture, if we love each other deeply above everything else, that love will cover a multitude of sins.

The way we love is often a product of the way we have been loved by our earthly parents. It's important to recognize that sometimes our earthly parents did not have the ability to love in the Biblical sense. The way to learn love is to look at the Father's love for His children. He loves us unconditionally. His perfect love casts out all fear.

When we live as loved ones there is no place for fear. When we love others as well as the Father loves us, we shine the light of Christ to those around us.

The Bible commands us to love one another deeply. In order to love someone, you don't have to like them, but we are told to love them deeply. Ask the Father for a greater understanding of His unconditional, never-ending love for you. Then you will be able to love those around you deeply and unconditionally.

PRAYER

Lord Jesus,

Thank You for Your unconditional love. Thank You that Your perfect love casts out all fear. Help me learn to receive Your love in all its purity. Help me love those around me deeply. Thank You that love covers a multitude of sin. Give me eyes of love and a burning desire to love those around me. Help me to step out, take risks, and love like I've never loved before. In the mighty name of Jesus. Amen.

The Quest of Abundant Life

. . . .

LAVISH LOVE

The best Bible truth that shows God's great love for us is found in John 3:16. Write the verse below. Meditate on it. Journal your thoughts below.

The best way to understand how to be loved and how to receive love is to understand the way of God's love. Read 1 Corinthians 13:4-8. Journal what love does and what love does not do. But rather than thinking of this in terms of human love, think of it in terms of how God pours out His love on you.

Read the same scripture, 1 Corinthians 13:4-8. Where you see the word, "love" and the word "it" as "it" refers to love, replace it with your name. This will help you understand how God loves you and how you are to love others.

Read Proverbs 10:12. Have you seen evidence of this verse in your life? Explain.

In John 15:12-13, Jesus says we are to love each other as He loves us. Jesus loves us so much that He laid down His life so that we could have forgiveness for sins and eternity with Him. Verse 13 talks about sacrificial love that we are to have towards others. To lay down our life for someone may mean we humble ourselves, we put them first, we listen to them. When have you had an opportunity to love someone sacrificially without expecting anything in return?

DAY 28

· ·

Complete Acceptance

*"Therefore welcome one another as Christ has
welcome you for the glory of God."*
Romans 15:7

Living welcomed and accepted are other keys of living the abundant life. Life, life and more life, nothing missing, nothing lacking, nothing broken.

In Romans 15:7 we learn that Christ has welcomed us. We have been adopted in His family and are seated at the right hand of the Father. We are no longer slaves to sin, but sons and daughters of the Most High God. Because of the work of Christ on the cross, we are worthy to take a seat at the Father's table and we are welcomed to join Him. Psalm 23 tells us that He prepares a table before us, in the presence of our enemies because He calls us "child."

As we learn and understand just how much we are loved, welcomed, and accepted, we are empowered in our identity. As we walk in our identity as welcomed ones, we rise in our authority and we rise as children of God and ambassadors of Christ. Today the Lord reminds you that He has welcomed you for His glory. He challenges you to welcome others.

The role of the evangelist is simply to welcome others into the Kingdom of God. If we know how welcomed we are, it becomes much easier to welcome others. Think about those in your family or friendship groups who do not know Christ. Begin to declare and decree over them that they are welcomed into the Kingdom regardless of their background or the situations or circumstances they may find themselves in. All for the glory of God.

PRAYER

Lord,

Thank You for welcoming me into Your family, Your arms and Your heart. Thank You for encouraging me to welcome others just as You have welcomed me. Empower me to identify those around me who would benefit from a warm welcome into Your Kingdom. My heart beats to see my family members and friends saved, so today I declare and decree a welcome over them. In the mighty name of Jesus. Amen.

The Quest of Abundant Life

. . . .

COMPLETE ACCEPTANCE

One of the complaints about Jesus made by the religious rulers is found in Luke 15:2. They muttered, "This man welcomes sinners and eats with them." Read Mark 2:17 to see "why" Jesus chose the "sinners" as His dinner companions.

Jesus has a heart big enough to love all people, young and old, big and small. Read Matthew 19:13-15. How does Jesus demonstrate His acceptance of children in this scripture?

In John 8:1-11, we read the story of Jesus and an adulterous woman. Read the story. Pause when you get to verse 11 and read it several times. The love of Jesus toward us is all encompassing, all accepting, and all available. Jesus says the same to us. "I do not condemn you, but I have a better life for you. Stand up, shake off the dust of sin from your life, go and sin no more." How does this verse resonate with the sin that tries to keep you tied down?

In Luke 23:32-43, Jesus showed the ultimate compassion, love, and acceptance to a man who was a criminal. Read the account. In verses 40-42, the man made a proclamation that brought salvation. Read Mark 5:34 to find out why and how the man received eternal life through these words spoken to Jesus.

God welcomes, accepts, and loves us because we are made in His image. He desires that no man shall perish. But in order to be a child of God, to be welcomed into His family, accepted as His child, and loved with the gift of eternal life, we must confess with our mouth and believe in our heart that God has raised Christ from the dead. For more, look at these verse from Romans (also known as the Romans Road) that help us better understand the way of salvation.

1. We are all sinners. Romans 3:10, Romans 3:23, Romans 6:23
2. Our hope is in Christ. Romans 5:8
3. We need to respond to Jesus. Romans 10:9-10, Romans 10:13
4. We receive His salvation. Romans 5:1-2, Romans 8:1

DAY 29

. . . .

Infectious Joy

"The joy of the Lord is my strength."
Nehemiah 8:10

We are called to be strong, to rise up and take the Kingdom by force. A key to doing this is found in our joy. The joy of the lord is our strength.

At the age of 28, I was diagnosed with terminal cancer. It was a difficult time, but the Lord imparted to me a supernatural, infectious joy that not only helped me through that season but bubbled out and overflowed to the world around me. I could not manufacture joy on my own, I was dependent upon the Lord to fill me with His joy.

Romans 15:13 reminds us that it is the Lord who fills us with all joy and peace in believing. True joy comes when we express heartfelt love, devotion, and gratitude to God. When we understand that God is at the center of all things, all situations, all circumstances and that He alone can bring about our greatest change, we are able to push anxiety and worry aside and live in contentment, trusting Him to work all things out for our good. Gradually, as our focus becomes set on the Lord and we trust Him more and more, our joy tanks are filled to overflowing.

Often in today's world and culture, we find ourselves on the serious road of life, going from one thing to the next, forgetting to stop and be thankful, to express gratitude, and to understand that God is in control and He promises to look after us in all things. When this joy wells up within, it naturally and supernaturally flows through us and into the lives of others.

We are called to be salt and life in the earth. If we are distracted, self-involved, and miserable, it will be a challenge to reach those around us. Today, the Lord wants to impart infectious joy to you, to give you an overflow of joy so that it will bubble out of you and touch the lives of those around you. Today the Lord is calling you to be saltier and brighter, to make a bigger impact in the world around you and therefore have access to the abundant life. May the joy of the Lord be your strength and cause you to rise up and impact the lives of those people around you.

PRAYER

Lord,

I receive your infectious joy. Even as I think of these words, I feel joy rising in my heart and spirit. This is the day the Lord has made, and I will rejoice and be glad in it. Help me remain in a posture to receive joy. Joy that breaks the chains that bind, joy that gives me stamina and strength to face the day, and joy to face the situations and circumstances that surround me. Thank you for your infectious joy. It is amazing. In the mighty name of Jesus. Amen.

The Quest of Abundant Life
. . . .
INFECTIOUS JOY

James 1:2 tells us to "Consider it pure joy when you face trials of many kinds." This is not saying that we must be excited or happy about tough times. This is to help us understand that we can profit in our spiritual growth and faith through the hard times. If you are in difficult situations or circumstances right now, ask the Lord to teach you how to persevere and how to grow through this season in life. If you have seen positive outcomes in difficult times, journal examples below:

Read Isaiah 9:3. Who fills us with joy and increases our joy?

Look up Proverbs 10:28. Who receives joy from the Lord?

In scripture, the apostle Peter encourages us with these words from 1 Peter 1:8-9, "Though you have not seen Him, you love Him; and even though you do not see Him now, you believe in Him and are filled with inexpressible and glorious joy, for you are receiving the goal of your faith, the salvation of your souls." Joy is available to all believers. If you find that you are not a joyful person, mark John's prayer from today's devotional and lift this request to God daily until He fills you with joy.

May the God of hope fill you with all joy and peace as you trust in Him, so that you may overflow with hope by the power of the Holy Spirit. Amen.
Romans 15:13

DAY 30

. . . .

Overflow

"Give and it will be given to you, a good measure, pressed down,
shaken together and running over will be poured into your lap.
For with the measure you use, it will be measured to you."
Luke 6:38

We have journeyed together for 30 days into the life of abundance, nothing missing, nothing lacking, and nothing broken. Let me tell you a secret. The reason we have walked into the abundant life is not for ourselves but so that we may overflow, bubble up, and pour out abundant life on everyone around us.

As Christians, we are called to reflect Christ and to be His ambassador. He came to earth, full of life, and He imparted that life to us so that we can impart and share that same life with others.

Today you are called to overflow, to enter into a generous space, giving thanks to the Lord for the life you have received throughout this journey. Ask Him to give you the courage and boldness to share this abundant life with everyone around you.

Life has been given to you, a good measure of life, pressed down and shaken together. Now the life that has been imparted into you is being released and is overflowing from you into those people around you.

Think about those you know who could use a new dose or sprinkling of life, whether family members, work colleagues, or friends. Bring them before your mind's eye and begin to declare and decree life over them in the name of Jesus.

PRAYER

Father,

Thank You for the journey we have taken together into the abundant life – life, life and more life, nothing missing, nothing lacking, and nothing broken. Thank You that as we have fixed our eyes upon You and have investigated the keys and tools for walking into the abundant life, the situations and circumstances that surround us have become smaller. Thank You for changing our perspective and empowering and enabling us to continue into the plans and purposes you have for us by imparting life. We receive Your abundant life today. In the mighty name of Jesus. Amen.

The Quest of Abundant Life
. . . .
OVERFLOW

When God created the heavens and the earth, He put the law of sowing and reaping in the DNA of the world's structure. For example, if we sow green beans, we will reap green beans. If we sow kindness, we will reap kindness from others. Read 2 Corinthians 9:6-8. How do you think this verse relates to the way we provide for others?

Based on the above verse, are there areas of your life where you need to improve what you are sowing so that your season of harvest will be richer? Describe:

Speaking of overflow, read Luke 6:45. How are the words that flow from your lips indicative of the condition of your heart?

Proverbs 10:11 gives us good reason to sow richly and to speak wisely. Write the verse below. What does it say the mouth of the righteous is to man?

Many times in scripture we are told to guard our hearts, to keep ourselves pure and free from the weight of sin. What is the reason given in Proverbs 4:23 for keeping our heart pure?

CONCLUSION

My prayer for you as you conclude this 30-day journey is that you will continue to lean into the Lord. Continue to seek His face and His guidance. There is no greater joy in life than to know and understand the promise of hope and eternal life we have because of the gift of salvation in Christ.

I encourage you to crawl into the lap of Father God and allow Him to bring wholeness to the wounds in your spirit brought on by the elements and woes of life. We have all been broken, we have all lost things we held dear, and we have all experienced lack. The Lord wants to bring restoration to your life - to restore everything broken, lost and lacking to the original plan He had for you before you were born.

He alone can do this. He alone can bring about this restoration. It will take time and it will take a willingness on your part to allow Him to lead you to this place of wholeness. But our God is the Great Physician, the Counselor, the Healer. As you grow in knowledge and understanding of Him, as you learn more and more about your identity in being His child, your heart and spirit will grow and become more in love with Him. Your desire will be to walk with Him more intimately and to allow Him to work through you.

Stay the course and make a go of it. He is faithful to His promises. Enjoy the journey and invite others to journey with you as you draw near to God and walk in His ways.

ABOUT THE AUTHOR

John Bell is a fresh prophetic voice of his generation. He has a burning desire to see the nations, generations, and denominations stand together in unity. He is an international speaker, chief encourager, bridge builder, and follower of Jesus Christ. John is deeply passionate about seeing people released and delivered from life's entrapments and stepping into their full potential and God-given identity.

John is co-founder of Healing Community Life Ministries. HCL's passion is to see vulnerable communities developed, healed, and transformed into Christian communities where families thrive and connect with God in exciting, real, and authentic ways.

To fuel his passion, John hosts a live interview program, "Sharing Life," which airs on Facebook and Youtube. Through this initiative, John dialogues with highly respected leaders in the five-fold ministry of the Church with the purpose of teaching, equipping, and encouraging believers to build bridges of community throughout the world.

Whether serving from their mission base in Colombia, South America, or their home base in Dallas, Texas, John and Susie continually build community, witnessing the healing power of God, demonstrating that healing happens when we do life together in genuine community.

To contact John for speaking engagements:

johnbellHCL@outlook.com
www.hclministries.com

More Books from John Bell

John is currently penning his life-story, "Cancer to Colombia." While residing in his mother country of England, at the age of 28, John received a diagnosis of terminal cancer with a 90-day life expectancy.

Through his death experience and subsequent return to earthly life, John goes into detail of how he heard the voice of the Lord speak into his heart. After being commissioned to take this second chance and live life to the full, John transitioned from a career in IT to a life of ministry.

John's testimony is one of victory over death, peace over chaos, and purpose over greed. It will be a great encouragement to the reader and a great gift to those who are seeking God in the midst of chaos, turmoil, or searching for the greater purpose of life.

Stay tuned for release date!

If this book has impacted you or brought you further questions or prayer requests, feel free to contact John directly at johnbellHCL@outlook.com.

Barbara,

My friend wrote this BOOK
and he truly captured what
our everyday approach to God
can be on so many topics.
I hope you enjoy the words
John penned as much as I
did.

Happy Belated Birthday.
Blessings,
Eileen